CW00688808

Arjan Singh, DFC

MARSHAL OF THE INDIAN AIR FORCE

Roopinder Singh

Rupa & Co

CONTENTS

CHAPTER ONE

The Ceremony

At Rashtrapati Bhavan, the period was post-colonial, but the setting very much colonial. On April 23, 2002, a select gathering of the elite of India—top brass from the Indian Air Force, the Navy and the Army, as well as political leaders, civil servants and diplomats —alighted from their vehicles in the forecourt of the official residence of the President of India.

They walked up the steps to the Ashoka Hall, past the six-feet tall soldiers of the President's Body Guard (PBG) dressed in their traditional ceremonial uniform and accoutrements that date back to 1890. The blue-and-gold ceremonial turban with the distinctive 'fan', a white longcoat with gold girdles, white buckskin gauntlets, white breeches and Napoleon boots with spurs, all looked distinctive indeed. Each soldier had in his hand the special 10-feet 9-inch-long bamboo cavalry lance made especially for the PBG, carried in stirrup lance buckets adorned with the red-and-white cavalry pennant. The wings of a trained combat parachutist, in gold, adorned the breast of each member of this elite unit, and medals glittered along with it.

The imposing four-storeyed Rashtrapati Bhavan has 340 rooms, but this day all eyes were fixed on the the Ashoka Hall. It was originally built as the State Ballroom and the assembled guests walked on the polished wooden floor. Many glanced at the ceiling with a painting in leather that depicted a royal hunting expedition in the centre and scenes from court life in the corners. It is a dark painting, and because of leather being the canvas, even the white has become brownish. The Persian-style painting was commissioned by Lady Willington when her husband was the Viceroy of India.

The Rashtrapati Bhavan

Those seated under this imposing canopy included Vice-President Krishan Kant, Prime Minister Atal Behari Vajpayee, Home Minister L. K. Advani, Defence Minister George Fernandes, External Affairs Minister Jaswant Singh, Air Chief Marshal Srinivasapuram Krishnaswamy and a large number of retired and serving military officers.

The PBG buglers sounded the fanfare from the central vestibules. Everybody in the Ashoka Hall stood up. The President of India, Kocheril Raman Narayanan, was escorted to the room by his aides-de-camp, dressed in the finery of their office. The band then played the National Anthem. The hall has seen many glittering events, but none as this one. On this day, the first-ever Marshal of the Indian Air Force was to be presented his baton by the President of India.

Marshal of the Indian Air Force Arjan Singh, DFC, had been named for this rarest of rare honours on January 26, 2002. This was the investiture ceremony for him and it meant a lot to everybody present, even though it had taken a while for it to happen.

A tall, handsome Sardar, sporting a milky white beard, wearing an Air Force uniform with five stars on the lapel, medals gleaming on his chest, marched up to the President with a sure stride. He belied his 83 years and stood straight before the Supreme Commander of the Indian armed forces.

The President of India, K.R.Narayanan presenting the 'Marshal's Baton'to Arjan Singh. The Marshal's Baton (right)

9

The President of India with Prime Minister Vajpayee, Arjan Singh and Defence Minister George Fernandes after the ceremony

In a departure from the customary investiture ceremony protocol, but in keeping with the importance of the occasion, the Defence Secretary, Mr Yogendra Narain, read the citation that concluded thus:

"His inspiring career, towering personality and distinguished reputation have endowed him with a unique stature in society and have earned him the respect of the nation. Even till date, he actively associates himself with various welfare activities of the Air Force as a father figure of the service, which he nurtured from its fledgling days.

"For his most outstanding and extraordinary service to the nation, the President of India is pleased to confer upon Air Chief Marshal Arjan Singh the rank of Marshal of the Indian Air Force."

The President acknowledged the salute of the veteran warrior. The baton was brought up on a velvet cushion. It was a magnificent creation that took the blue from the sky and had the glitter of gold gilding.

The President handed the baton to Marshal of the Air Force Arjan Singh, who saluted him again. The President shook hands with him. They clasped each other's hands for several minutes thereafter as press photographers and television cameramen asked them to pose over and over again.

Beaming with happiness was the lady of the day, Mrs Teji Arjan Singh, in a russet organza sari. She has stood by her husband through the eventful years with grace and charm that have become legendary. Sitting next to her in a white embroidered outfit was their daughter Asha. The National Anthem was played once more and the President and his guests retired to the Banquet Hall.

During tea at the Banquet Hall, adjoining the Ashoka Hall, the mood was informal. Life-size portraits of past Presidents of India seemed to look upon the historic event approvingly as Marshal

Arjan Singh was greeted by a large number of his well-wishers. The Prime Minister and the President gracefully conceded the centre stage to the 83-year-old pilot, who proudly wore the Distinguished Flying Cross, Padma Vibhushan, and a host of other medals.

Standing Amrita, Arjan Singh, and (sitting) Arvind, Asha with Arjan's mother Kartar Kaur, 1962

This was his day. It was also a day for the Indian Air Force to be proud of. An icon of the service had been honoured. India's elite was there to commemorate the event and pay their respects to Marshal of the Indian Air Force Arjan Singh.

Who is Arjan Singh? What has he done to deserve this singular honour and adulation? He fought three major wars during his tenure with the Air Force and built the Indian Air Force virtually from scratch. He then went on diplomatic assignments to Switzerland, the Vatican and Kenya; was a Member of the Minorities Commission; and served as the Lieut-Governor of Delhi. Distinguished public service was balanced with his family life. As he recollects: "I have always been a family man—no matter how busy I have been, I have always managed to take time out for my family."

The Marshal of the Indian Air Force had managed to live a life in which he incorporated various roles—he had originally received a King's Commission in the Indian Air Force, and had gone on to serve Independent India well. Commissioned by King George VI, honoured by both the British and the Indians, a superb flyer who is now a father figure, a soldier and a diplomat, this is no ordinary man.

One cannot but think of the beginnings of Arjan Singh when he was born to Kishan Singh and Kartar Kaur on April 15, 1919, at Kohali village in Lyallpur, now in Pakistan.

CHAPTER TWO

Pre-flight

Risaldar Bhagwan Singh, Arjan Singh's grandfather, had moved to Lyallpur district from Amritsar district since the land there was well irrigated by canals. This was a part of the migration in the late 1800s when people moved from eastern Punjab to the western districts because the irrigation system developed by the British was more efficient. Often a number of families from a particular village would migrate and form a new village that would share its name with the original one. Thus, the village in Lyallpur district was an offshoot of Kohali village, near Amritsar. Lyallpur, now in Pakistan, is called Faislabad. Other members of Risaldar Bhagwan Singh's family also settled in the village.

Bhagwan Singh's son Kishan Singh did not stay in the village. He studied in Lyallpur and then earned his B.Sc degree at Khalsa College, Amritsar, where the famous G. A. Wathen was Principal. He then went to England soon after Arjan Singh's birth in 1919 and spent four years in Edinburgh University, Scotland, where he studied civil engineering. On the way back, his ship docked at

Arjan Singh (standing last row, third from left) with fellow students at S.N. Das Gupta Coaching College, Lahore 1937-38

15

Colombo and he became an engineer in Ceylon Railways. "I was in school at that time and I remember that I used to get passes that entitled even us children to travel First Class. I used to go there every holiday. He served in Ceylon Railways for a long time," remembers Arjan Singh.

Arjan Singh has fond memories of his grandfather. He was still a child when his grandfather died: "I was young when he passed away and I remember that the funeral procession had a band in it, since the custom those days was that if someone died at a ripe old age, the death was celebrated with a band. We weren't landlords, but we were quite comfortably placed."

Asked to recollect his childhood, Arjan Singh says: "I was always fascinated by aeroplanes. I first saw them when they flew over our village near Lyallpur *en route* from Lahore to Karachi and I knew that I wanted to be in those planes."

He studied in the Government High School, Montgomery, which was the better school in the region. He particularly remembers his schoolmate Justice Manmohan Singh Gujral, who now lives in Chandigarh. Arjan Singh learned to swim in a canal that was located between his family's farm and the school. That stood him in good stead because he captained the school, college, university and the provincial swimming teams. He held two long-distance national records in freestyle swimming—one mile and half mile.

Manmohan Gujral and Arjan Singh joined Government College, Lahore, together. He stayed in a hostel called the Quadrangle since it was cheaper and near the swimming pool. He would swim 20-30 lengths every morning and then attend classes. Professor Ward from Cambridge was his favourite professor, but he lost contact with him after leaving the

Catching the 'one-fifteen' train from King's Cross, (London)

A weekend in the country, during training at Cranwell

college. "My wife and I went especially to Cambridge in 1950 to trace him, but we could not, even though we went to his last-known address. A lady living in the next house told us that he went to fight in World War II and never returned." He also

17

RAF Flying College, Cranwell (Hockey 1st XI - 1939), Arjan Singh (vice-captain) and Prithipal Singh (standing right)

remembers Professor G. D. Sondhi, who became the Principal later. Sondhi guided the students in swimming and *kabaddi*. He also recalls Professor Kasim, his tutor at the college.

Arjan Singh is proud of his college colours in swimming, *gatka*, athletics and *kabaddi*, but he never neglected his studies. He earned an Inter-Art degree, FA, for which he also studied mathematics and physics. When he was in the fourth year of college, he was selected for the Indian Air Force and had to leave college a few months before he finished the BA degree. Along with six or seven students from Lahore, he had taken the defence examination at Metcalf House, Civil Lines, Delhi. Five were selected. They included Prithipal Singh who belonged to the royal house of Patiala.

In 1938, travelling to England was quite enjoyable. A Peninsular and Orient (P&O) liner sailed across the high seas, passing through Aden, the Suez Canal and Gibraltar. Prithipal Singh, Arjan Singh, and another cadet from India, took such a liner and reached England for their training. "When we joined Cranwell, Prithipal was number one, but by the time we passed out, I came first." They were the only foreigners; while Arjan Singh had to put in an extra effort at

As vice-captain Arjan Singh (sitting on right) with the college athletics team in 1939

Auro Tutor aircraft (left) for initial training and advance Trainer Audax at Cranwell

speaking English, Prithipal Singh, who had been brought up by British governesses, did not have any problem at all. If a word was mispronounced, the instructor made the necessary correction and suggested a remedy for it; the emphasis in training was on the development of one's character in order to become a good officer. The training involved not just flying, but much more than that. Among those who left lasting impressions on Arjan Singh were Sergeant Harries, the flying instructor, and Squadron Leader D. A. Boyle, the Chief Flying Instructor, who was later knighted and became Marshal of the Royal Air Force.

Life at Cranwell involved studying a lot of mathematics, physics, electronics and engineering without any social life when the college was in session. During weekends, they went to London to meet Indian friends, though often the British cadets would invite the Indians to their homes on weekends. They remained in touch with each other for decades, especially Marshal of the Royal Air Force Sir John Grandy, GCB, GCVO, KBE, DSO, and the late Marshal of the Royal Air Force Lord Samuel Charles Elworthy, KG, GCB, CBE, DSO, LVO, DFC, AFC, who was a New Zealander. Both were his opposite numbers when he was Chief of Air Staff.

Arjan Singh has kept his flying log book in which his entire flying career is noted. An early entry shows the meticulous care they exercised in those days. When Boyle noticed that blue and black inks had been used for making entries in the log book, he observed: "By using the same ink and the same pen, you would improve the appearance of the log book." You also notice that "Flight Cadet A.

Vice Captain Cranwell Aquatic Team (1939). Events were freestyle and water polo as centre-forward

Singh" got an "Average" in flying, which rose to "Above Average" on December 22, 1939. He was awarded colours in swimming, athletics and hockey and was the Vice-Captain of the teams for these sports.

When the Second World War began in Europe in September 1939, their training was cut short due to the shortage of pilots in the Air Force and they were commissioned in December, 1939. There was a shortage of pilots everywhere—in the Royal Air Force in Britain

B Sqn Royal Air Force College, Cranwell (England) in 1939

and the Indian Air Force in India, which had only one squadron at Ambala. Prithipal Singh and Arjan Singh were the last two officers to join the squadron in January 1940. This Indian squadron had been formed on April 1, 1933 at Drigh Road, Karachi by the first batch of airmen, who were called the Hawai Sepoys and a few officers (including Subroto Mukherjee, who later

No.1 Squadron Crest. Its personnel are called 'tigers' and their motto is 'Itbad Mein Shakti'

became the first Indian Air Chief) and was commanded by an RAF officer. Originally, it had four Westland Wapitis (a fabric bomber/reconnaissance biplane, typical of the RAF aircraft during the inter-war period). The joining of these two officers brought the squadron to its full strength in 1940.

CHAPTER THREE

Top-Gun

From Ambala, a flight of No. 1 Squadron went to Karachi and then to the North West Frontier Province (NWFP). This was close to the Durand Line; the terrain dictated the style of fighting much as it does in today's conflict in that area. There were no big targets that could be hit. The Pathans hid in caves and valleys and took pot-shots at prowling aircraft, occasionally managing to disable some. Arjan Singh also was the target once.

The aircraft they flew were quite elementary in design and technology. They flew the Westland Wapiti, and the Hawker Audax (a variant of the Hart for Army co-operation role).

To hear the story from Arjan Singh of how he once had to crash-land is to learn the process of initiation into the business of war. "At that time, the British idea was not to take over the area and have complete administrative control, but to give a live target and operational training to the soldiers. My experience is that unless you see the bullets coming towards you and some hitting you, you

A Wafiti aircraft flown by Arjan Singh over mountains of NWFP (now in Pakistan)

A Distinguished Trio — Squadron Leaders Arjan Singh, Mehar (Baba) Singh and Prithipal Singh (l to r)

don't have the experience of war. The first few times that you have these bullets hitting the aircraft, you are afraid. I was afraid.

"In 1940, my Hawker Audax was shot down in the NWFP by the Pathans. I crashed in a dry hilly stream where a fight was going on between the British/Indian troops, on the one side, and the Pathans, on the other. My gunner, Gulam Ali, was injured in the crash. I stayed with him till we both could be evacuated. Gulam Ali has eventually settled down in Germany. I was in touch with him until a few years ago." The incident is dismissed casually. "But it was not much, within two weeks I was flying again—in the same area. Our fighting in the NWFP, I think, prepared us for the fight, later on, against the Japanese." Arjan Singh maintains that operations over the mountains and valleys of the NWFP prepared him to face

Squadron Leader K. K. (Jumbo) Majumdar DFC and Bar

the tougher war against the Japanese during 1944 on the eastern front. He says: "One always has much fear at the beginning but after a few operational sorties, it becomes a routine affair and the fear almost disappears." He flew a total of 128 hours in operations over the Frontier Province.

Arjan Singh had a long tenure in No. 1 Squadron. He had joined in 1940 and, except for a few months, he had been in the squadron all the time. He served as Adjutant, and then Flight Commander. This was unusual, since officers are generally shifted after promotions.

The Indian Air Force was equipped with the famous Hawker Hurricane of the 'Battle of Britain' fame in 1942 and most of its squadrons were given the aircraft during that year. This all-metal aircraft was sturdy and reliable. As Arjan Singh remembers: "I operated this aircraft on the North West Frontier Province (and later) against the Japanese and it never let me down even once." Squadron Leader Arjan Singh was made CO in September, 1943 in Kohat, now in Pakistan.

It was as a Squadron Leader that he first met Teji, the lady who became his wife. He had flown from Kohat to Delhi to attend a

Flight Lt. Arjan Singh with members of his flight. From left — Ibrahim, Ratnagar, A. Singh, Henry and Murcot

Squadron Commanders' Conference on November 22, 1943, in which his old class fellow, Squadron Leader Prithipal Singh, and the legendary Squadron Leader Mehar Singh and Squadron Leader K. K. (Jumbo) Majumdar were also participating. (Unfortunately, Prithipal Singh and Majumdar died in 1945 in Hurricane crashes and Mehar Singh died in a civilian aircraft crash after retiring from the IAF.).

In Delhi, Arjan Singh was staying in the house of Partap Singh, who was a builder and partner of Sir Sobha Singh, one of the most prominent builders of Delhi. Partap Singh had also studied in Arjan Singh's *alma mater*, Government College, Lahore. As Teji recalls, "The late Air Marshal Subroto Mukherjee had requested my father, who was a good friend, to accommodate various officers in Delhi for the conference."

With his mechanics Daruwala and Kalsi

The pretty, young and petite Teji and the tall, handsome Sardar met, and the rest, as they say, is history. They continued meeting each other, often playing a game of table tennis. To quote Arjan Singh, he "waited for her to grow up." A Pontiac played its part. "It was a huge car, and I thought that he had bought it to impress me," remembers Teji, who was studying in the Convent of Jesus and Mary then.

Arjan Singh had bought his steel-grey Pontiac when he was posted in Risalpur, near Peshawar. He had actually wanted a Chevrolet,

With his pilots Hafiz and Sircar near a water-logged Hurricane at Imphal Airfield in 1944

Playing volleyball at Imphal, 1944

but at that time they were being sold at a premium since they were coveted by the Pathans of the NWFP. The Pontiac cost him Rs 7,000. Before he bought the car, he rode an 'Indian' motorcycle purchased for a grand sum of Rs 250, which was quite a lot, considering that his salary in those days was a mere Rs. 325 per month. The Indian was the first commercially marketed gasoline-powered motorcycle in America.

The bike or the car were far from his mind when Squadron Leader Arjan Singh went to Imphal in 1943 as Squadron Commander. War clouds were looming over the horizon. The situation there was precarious since the Japanese strategy in World War II was to enter India through the east. They had already conquered South-East Asia, including Burma, and had laid a siege to the Imphal Valley. The only land route—Dimapur, Kohima, Imphal—had been cut off by the Japanese. All the forces in the valley were supplied by transport aircraft, mostly by the American Air Force, diverted from the other task of supplying the forces of Chiang Kai-Shek "over

"To Arjan Singh from Baldwin — Am delighted to tell you that you have been awarded the D. F. C" — (Ops Immediate)

Admiral Lord Mountbatten, Supreme Commander, South East Asia Command, pinning the Distinguished Flying Cross medal on Arjun Singh at Imphal in June 1944

The squadron celebration after the award. Air officer commanding 221 Group Air Commodore S. F. Vincent is lying on the ground with him

the Hump" of the 18,000 to 22,000 ft. above sea level high mountain ranges between Assam and China.

The squadron was stationed in the valley. It played a major role in helping the Indian/British Army fighting in the valley to withstand the siege and overpower the Japanese forces. They attacked Japanese troops and supply lines, though there was not much aerial combat. There was a healthy rivalry between the RAF and the IAF and this gave the IAF a chance to prove that they were as good as the RAF, if not better, at fighting against well-established enemies. This they did by flying long and dangerous hours and relentlessly hitting the enemy troops.

IAF Sqn Cdrs' Meeting New Delhi, 1943

Fifteen and a dog on Willis Jeep! L to R : Prabhakar, Hafiz 'Munnu Mian', Rishi, 'Koko', 'Doc' Herbert, Maj Williams, Skipper, DP, 'Tutu' Amber, 'Raja', Khema Kak, Bonzo, 'Nifty' Pandit, 'Pop' Rao, Gupi Gupta, Tallu' Talwar

Air Chief P. C. Lal in his book *My Years with the IAF*, published in 1986, says: "The first person to actually see the Japanese in the northern part of Imphal was Squadron Leader Ajran Singh. He had been on a sortie, attacking the Japanese elsewhere and he was coming back to base in the afternoon flying his aircraft solo at that time. Coming back to circuit and land at his base, he saw on a hilltop overlooking the airfield a number of men in a strange

A Japanese tank damaged by air attack, Arjan Singh is seen extreme left

uniform that did not resemble any uniform or any men of the Indian Army. So he went close to have a look and recognised them as Japanese troops.... He immediately called his entire squadron on his own initiative. The other aircraft that were on the ground were also made ready to go. He was the first to attack the Japanese, who had actually arrived on the outskirts of Imphal." Documents published later have shown that this attack by the whole squadron i.e. 16 aircraft was the turning point and final reversal of their ambitious plan to capture the valley.

P. C. Lal, Arjan Singh's successor as Chief of Air Staff, further writes: "His leadership had a distinct style: quiet courage, no flamboyance, firmness with a ready smile. He and his boys were the heroes of Imphal. He had done a great job."

The leadership of Squadron Leader Arjan Singh was noticed and he was given the immediate award of the Distinguished Flying Cross (DFC) in May, 1944, by Lord Louis Mountbatten, Supreme Allied Commander of South-East Asia during World War II. The event was commemorated with a small ceremony at the airfield itself. Lord Mountbatten addressed the squadron while standing on the wing of Squadron Leader Arjan Singh's Hurricane and pinned the DFC on his chest. "I was dressed in my jungle fatigues,"

A Japanese aircraft damaged by No.1 Squadron attack in Burma 1944

						TOTALS BROUGHT FORWARD
:H	26	HURRICANE	403	SELF	—	TAC/R UKHRUL — KOHIMA ARE
	28	"	"	"		TAC/R JESSAMI
	29	"	"	"		STRAFFING — PUKHAO

A Flying Logbook entry, showing air attack casualties of Japanese troops, 1944

remembers the Marshal. "It did not come as a complete surprise. He gave us about two hours notice, we gathered some officers and airmen of the squadron, but we did not stop the operations even then. For a young man to get such a medal in front of his own squadron is a great satisfaction. I was a part of the squadron, at Imphal and they were a part of me.

DFC - Distinguished Flying Cross

Even now, I am in touch with at least five of the people who were with me in Imphal, three of them are Airmen and two are officers."

Pilots depend on ground technical staff to keep the planes in good condition. Arjan Singh fondly recollects the contribution of the technical wizard who looked after the planes—Group Captain Ram

```
1.15
1.30
 .30        Total   ☒ Jap Casualties   Officers = 14   O. ranks 217
```

Singh, MBE (Member of the British Empire). He belonged to Sansarpur village, near Jalandhar in Punjab, which is famous for producing legendary hockey players. He was the first person to join as Hawai Sepoy.

In all, his squadron got nine DFCs—which is quite a record. No other squadron, whether Indian or British, got so many DFCs on the Burma Front. But the cost was sadly high—out of the 21 pilots who originally went from Kohat to Imphal, only five returned. Two of the DFC-winners, Air Vice-Marshal A. R. (Nifty) Pandit and Group Captain (Nanu) Shitoley were among the first to congratulate the Marshal of the Indian Air Force when his new rank was announced. Following such a long stint on the front, the squadron was moved and its chief given a peace-time posting.

CHAPTER FOUR

𝒯op 𝐵rass

Arjan Singh was then shifted as Squadron Leader, Operations, with a comfortable office in the South Block overlooking Rajpath. This was the seat of power, the heart of Lutyen's Delhi, but he was not destined to stay in this position for long as he replaced Wing Commander K. K. (Jumbo) Majumdar, who was killed in a crash in Lahore on February 17, 1945, while flying a Hawker Hurricane on an aerobatic demonstration sortie for the Indian Air Force Display Flight (AFDF). This legendary pilot had been awarded a Bar to his

Squadron Commanders of the I.A.F. get-together in New Delhi, Sept 1943. Sqn. Ldr. Mukerjee is sitting second from right, front row

DFC just a month earlier, becoming the first and the only Indian to be so decorated during World War II.

AFDF had been constituted for touring the country to conduct aerobatic shows and displays to attract and bring to the public notice the Indian Air Force's exploits. After Jumbo Majumdar's death, Arjan Singh was posted to AFDF as Wing Commander, but only for a few months. He was subsequently selected for training at the RAF Staff College in England, the first person to be so chosen.

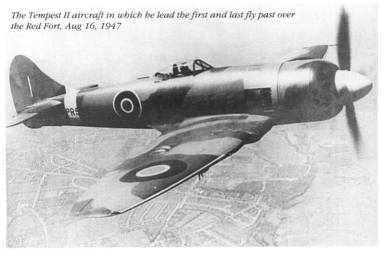

The Tempest II aircraft in which he lead the first and last fly past over the Red Fort, Aug 16, 1947

This course lasted a year or so. After his return, he was promoted to Group Captain on August 15, 1947, and given the command of the Ambala Air Force station.

India became Independent and Group Captain Arjan Singh led, in a Tempest, a formation flight over the Red Fort on the August 16, 1947, when Prime Minister Jawaharlal Nehru unfurled the National Flag over the ramparts of the seat of Mughal power, the Red Fort. That was the first and the last time that a fly-past was conducted over the Red Fort. The idea was later abandoned because of the fear of bird hits damaging an aircraft and causing a crash in the congested area. He has also led the fly-past on Republic Day over Rajpath, five times—as Air Commodore and Air Vice-Marshal. It used to be a grand affair, particularly in the early days, and one of the Marshal's fond memories is of the time they put up 110 aircraft for the fly-past at various heights, flying at speeds varying from 100 to 400 miles per hour.

Arjan Singh and Teji, on their wedding day, Feb 15, 1948, New Delhi

The family was already living in India, before Partition, but Arjan Singh's father's ancestral land, and his own land had been in the area that now became Pakistan. Kishan Singh had left his job in Ceylon Railways because there was discrimination against Indians. Air Commodore Mehar Singh as well as Group Captain Arjan Singh had been allocated land in the Terai region of Uttar Pradesh, which his father started looking after. This was not the only land they had. "We owned land in Pakistan and were allotted 80 acres of land in Churwali village, near Adampur, Punjab after Partition. I

43

was also allotted a *pucca* house. Kartar Singh, a good man, used to look after the land and when I sold the land, I gave the house to him. I sold off the land because I could not take care of it as I was in service, a full-time occupation. In fact, when I told Sardar Swaran Singh (the External Affairs Minister of India then), in whose constituency my land fell, how much I had sold it for, he chided me for selling it below the market rate." Surat Singh (Arjan Singh's brother who was eight years younger and had a career in civil aviation before he left it to take care of the lands) and their father looked after the land in Terai.

Arjan Singh may have sold off his extensive land holdings, but he is still a *jat* at heart and the love for land still makes him spend his

The Spitfire — the famous aircraft of the Battle of Britain

Sundays at his farm just outside Delhi. Perhaps it reminds him of the peace and tranquillity, the lush green fields he saw when he was still commanding Ambala station. He had just married Teji, who was then just shy of 18 years. The marriage took place in the Janpath house of Sir Sobha Singh, one of the builders of New Delhi, on February 15, 1948.

A photograph taken soon after their wedding

Those were different times— the pilots from the squadron went to Air Marshal Sir Thomas W. Elmhirst, and sought permission to close the station for two days since their CO was getting married. He agreed and also gave them permission to keep up their flying training which involved flying over Delhi, too.

"Soon after the wedding ceremony, there were 12 Harvard aircraft flying in the formation of A and T in the sky over us. My husband was furious and exclaimed, 'My God! They are going to have me court marshalled on my wedding day!' But Air Marshal Mukherjee, Air Marshal (Aspy Merwan) Engineer and Air Marshal Elmhirst, the Chief of Air Staff, were at the wedding. 'Cool down, old chap! I authorised it,' Air Marshal Elmhirst interjected.

Teji recollects how as the CO's spouse she went to the Ambala Air Force Station where she was the youngest wife, and ladies much older than her sought her advice! A senior Air Force officer's wife is expected to look after the welfare of other officers' and airmen's families, and she was soon in the thick of all this. Life at a station in peacetime is a good one, with a small social circle and the usual rounds of welfare work and parties.

But life wasn't all that uneventful. Teji remembers an incident about five months after their wedding when they were driving on the GT road and saw a truck full of bales of cotton on fire. Arjan Singh and his old bearer went to rescue the people in spite of the fire and it was only after their clothes caught fire that they stopped. "You should have seen them, leaping into the flames! Anything could have happened. I was so scared! I lived this nightmare for years, I would wake up in the middle of the night, replaying the horror," she says. The intervention took its toll, both were singed though the bearer was severely burnt and was hospitalised at

Panipat for over a month, during which the Singhs would visit him often.

Promoted to Air Commodore in 1949, Arjan Singh took over as the Air Officer Commanding, Operational Command. It is well known at Western Air Command that Arjan Singh had the distinction of having the longest tenure as the AOC of the Operational Command, from 1949 to 1952 and again from 1957 to 1960.

It was in 1949 that their first daughter Amrita was born. Three years later her brother Arvind Singh was born and the youngest, Asha, followed another three years later. The girls studied in their mother's *alma mater*, Convent of Jesus and Mary, and then at Lady Sri Ram College, both in Delhi. Arvind studied in St Columba's, School, Delhi. He then studied history at St Stephens College, Delhi. By this time, the family was in Switzerland and since they now had access to foreign exchange, he joined the London School of Economics. He got a PhD from the University of Chicago and has settled in the USA with his wife Cynthia. They have two children Vikram and Priya. Arvind teaches business administration at the University of Arizona.

Amrita was married to Jai Inder Singh, an IAS officer, but, unfortunately, passed away in 1999, just short of her 50th birthday.

Standing in the cockpit of a Hurricane before a flight

They have two children, Sameer Singh and Maya. The loss was devastating for the family and both Arjan Singh and his wife were taken seriously ill that year. The youngest daughter Asha lives with her parents and runs a boutique in Delhi.

The children were very young when, in 1960, Air Vice-Marshal Arjan Singh went to England for the one-year course at Imperial Defence College (now called Royal College of Defence Studies), in London. During the break at IDC in August/September he went to the USA and Canada, where he got good exposure to the

Briefing pilots for an operational flight at Imphal in 1944

operational procedures of their air forces and also met a number of officers, some of whom became good friends. He says that he was surrounded by highly decorated officers and "felt like a mini" out there. After this course, which prepares officers for higher postings, he held various senior appointments at Air Headquarters. He was Air Officer, Administration (1961), Deputy Chief of the Air Staff (1963) and subsequently Vice-Chief of the Air Staff.

He was in the Air Headquarters when the Chinese invasion in 1962 took place. As Arjan Singh recalls: "It was not because of the

Teji pointing to the 'extra' stripe on the day he become Air Chief Marshal in 1966

fighting ability of our soldiers that we suffered, it was because of bad leadership in the Army and political interference." It was decided that the Air Force should not play a fighting role in this war, because once the air forces get involved, it ceases to be a limited engagement. As it turned out, the Air Force did play a 'non-fighting' role in logistic support and in evacuating wounded soldiers. Even though he was not in command, Arjan Singh says the Air Force was prepared to fight and the Chinese advance would have been much restricted had the Air Force also participated in that operation.

Arjan Singh took over as Chief of the Air Staff (CAS) on July 15, 1964, and within a year came the most testing time of his life.

Pakistani forces infiltrated into Kashmir in August, 1965, and later attacked the Chhamb-Jaurian sector with regular army formations on September 1, 1965. It was a fierce attack in which a Pakistani

Speaking on the All India Radio, 1966

force of two infantry brigades and two armoured regiments were involved. The 3rd Mahar battalion bore the brunt of the attack. They were supported by a squadron of tanks of the 20th Lancers, but there was no artillery support since the enemy shelling had damaged and dislocated some of our artillery.

The Army in Kashmir sent a request for air support at 11 am. General J. N. Chaudhury, Army Chief at the time, asked the Air Chief if the Air Force could help. Both the service chiefs went to the Defence Minister, Y. B. Chavan, who gave the permission within a few minutes. He asked the CAS: "Can you do it?"

As he recalls, the CAS replied: "We just can. If you give orders now, we may be able to attack before night." The urgent note was justified because it was 4 pm when the order was issued and the Indian Air Force lacked night vision equipment and the attack would be launched in twilight, which would be risky.

Chavan gave the orders, though, as he recorded in his diary: "Had no time to consult ECC or Prime Minister. Time was a vital factor. Took decision on their (the chiefs) advice and asked them to go ahead." Chavan maintained a diary and his records have been printed in *Debacle to Revival: Y B Chavan as Defence Minister 1962-65* by R D Pradhan, the Defence Minister's aide.

The air attack was launched from Pathankot, near the border of Jammu and Kashmir that day. Vampires of World War II vintage were also used for the sorties in addition to Mysteres and Gnats.

Inspecting a parade

The first wave of four Vampires took of at 1719 hrs, as soon as they got orders. They inflicted considerable damage on the enemy tanks, though they also attacked, by mistake, some of our own Army positions and troops. One Vampire was lost to ground fire in this attack. The second wave of four Vampires was attacked by Sabre jets which were vastly superior in performance and armament, and three Vampires were lost in that attack, with one managing to escape. The fourth wave did not encounter any aircraft and attacked enemy troops, armour and vehicles.

Arjan Singh recalls: "We were able to attack Pakistani troops but, unfortunately, hit some of our own troops as well. We lost four Vampire aircraft, but the whole operation was a major success.

The President Dr. Radhakrishnan and Defence Minister Y.B. Chavan at the Beating Retreat, 1966

Damaged and captured Pakistani tanks at Khem Karan, near Amritsar

Though planning and execution could have been better, the objective of stopping Pakistan's advance was achieved."

This was the beginning. The war escalated and the Indian Army and Indian Air Force performed well as can be judged from some of the headlines in the various newspapers during the period as well as from Chavan's diary:

The Indian Express on September 2, 1965 reported: "IAF Planes go into Action, 10 Pakistani Patton Tanks Destroyed. Enemy Offensive Repulsed". Chavan's observations on Septembers 3, 1965 were: "This day began with a gift from the IAF. CAS came to my residence with the news that the IAF, in the morning air battle, had shot down an F-86 in the Chhamb sector...." Three days later, the Defence Minister told Parliament: "The House is undoubtedly proud of the performance of our boys in the Air Force who have destroyed several Pakistani Sabre jets."

On September 12, 1965 Chavan wrote: "CAS is given OK for Peshawar. When he is asked to go ahead on a new task, CAS walks as a dancing bird. A real fighting Sikh: and yet how soft and gentle." Ten days later, he was to say: "Army and Air Force have become now for us the symbols of our national pride and glory. A

With Y B Chavan looking at first PAF Sabre casuality in 1965, now in the IAF Museum at the Palam Air Force Station

Prime Minister Lal Bahadur Shastri standing on a captured Pakistani tank, 1965

great day for me. A great day for Chaudhury (the Army Chief) and Arjan Singh ...Air Marshal Arjan Singh is a jewel of a person; quietly efficient and firm, unexcitable but a very able leader."

During the war, the Indian Air Force penetrated deep into Pakistani territory and attacked military targets around Peshawar, Quetta, Rawalpindi, Sargodha and other Pakistani cities. As many as 72 trains and many vehicles were attacked, disrupting the Pakistani army's supply lines. They scrupulously followed Prime Minister Lal

Bahadur Shastri's instructions to attack military targets only.

As the war progressed, the pilots' confidence increased. Initially, there had been some doubts about the ability of the indigenous Gnats against the highly sophisticated American-built Sabres, but even those flying the Gnats showed a lot of élan, particularly after they shot down two Sabres of the Pakistani Air Force in the initial days of war. *The Statesman* on September 4, 1965 gave a banner headline: "Two Pakistani Sabre Jets Downed".

It was a short war. Mainly under international pressure, a UN brokered cease-fire was announced on September 23, 1965. The Army had conquered considerable Pakistani territory, and the war had seen the biggest tank battles since World War II. Yet the

With Prime Minister Indira Gandhi at the Commanders' Conference, 1968

fighting men were itching for more. However, a stalemate in land fighting had been reached. As Arjan Singh says: "The 1965 war was too short for us. I was disappointed when the ceasefire was announced because in my opinion the war was going on well for us. We were able to attack every target in Pakistan, while they could not send planes beyond Ambala! They could not even reach Delhi, let alone Mumbai or Ahmedabad. We had minimal casualties in the Air Force."

His wife Teji recalls his unhappiness when he came back home: "You should have seen his face. So unhappy! I asked him what had happened and he said that the war was over at a time when the things were very comfortable for the Air Force. They had enough ammunition,

The whole sequence of shooting down a Pakistani Sabre by a Gnat in 1965 war, taken by a cine-camera fixed in the nose of an aircraft

Getting out of a Mig 21, after a flight

and the pilots were doing well." He recollects how the President, Dr Sarvepalli Radhakrishnan, said that he had been told that the Army was bogged down in its advance into Pakistan.

Other accounts suggest that even the Army was not in a mood for a cease-fire, as it had captured substantial Pakistani territory, though,

In conversation with PM Lal Bahadur Shastri, 1965

of course, its supply lines were stretched because an invasion takes a lot more resources than defence. Defence Minister Chavan had also supported the military stand.

Both the Army Chief and the Air Chief were awarded the Padma Vibhushan. Thus, the CAS got the award at the age of 46. His rank was raised to that of Air Chief Marshal by a grateful nation, although he says: "Personally, I didn't think that I deserved either of them, since I wasn't quite satisfied with what we did in the 1965 war. Given some more time, we would have done far better."

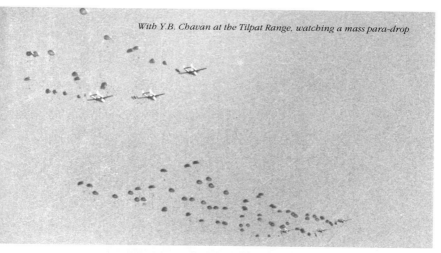

With Y.B. Chavan at the Tilpat Range, watching a mass para-drop

Receiving the Padma Vibhushan from the President

The citation of the Padma Vibhushan dated November 24, 1965, would suggest that he is being too modest. It reads:

"A fearless and able pilot himself, Air Marshal Arjan Singh, Chief of the Air Staff, India, has a distinguished record of service. As a chief of India's Air Force, he has worked assiduously for its expansion and reorganisation. By his personal example, he has infused in the Airmen a high sense of discipline and devotion to duty.

"During the recent armed conflict with Pakistan, when the enemy Air Force launched attacks on our airfields and ground forces in several theatres of war, it became necessary for our Air Force to go into action not only repelling the attacks and striking at enemy's bases, but also providing close support to our ground forces. The action required detailed planning and coordination of a highly complicated nature. The tactical deployment of personnel and aircraft had to be done with meticulous care, particularly when the enemy was using highly sophisticated aircraft and equipment. Air Marshal Arjan Singh met the situation with rare courage and

With airmen at an Air Force Station

The heroes of yesteryear meet the C.A.S.

determination, and coordinated the operations with professional skill of a very high order. The brilliant results achieved during his operations, in which heavy losses were inflicted on the enemy's fighting potential, including armour, aircraft and airfields, are standing testimony to the outstanding qualities of leadership displayed by Air Marshal Arjan Singh."

Teji has an interesting account to offer about the event. She recalls how they were in Calcutta when they were woken up at about 2.30 am by a phone call from his staff officer. Arjan Singh answered the phone. When she asked if another war had taken place, he said no, he had been awarded the Padma Vibhushan, and promptly went back to sleep!

He had put in two years of service as Air Marshal and the tenure for the new rank was three years. Thus Arjan Singh stayed the longest in the top saddle of the Air Force.

After the war, it was time for stock taking. The biggest losses of the Indian Air Force were in Pathankot, and this was a failure of command on the part of the officers there. "After the 1965 war, I asked two Air Commodores and a couple of Group Captains to put in their resignation, as well as some other people. I told them that they could continue receiving their pension if they resigned; otherwise I would have them dismissed as they had not done well and could not continue in service. Years later, when I was in Switzerland, some of them wrote to me saying that they were sorry that they had let me down. An Air Commodore settled in Pune said that he felt very sad that he had let me down. You have to maintain discipline. If someone has done wrong, punish him, if he has done well, reward him."

After the war, he advocated a policy of greater self reliance. This resulted in a number of new projects for manufacturing aircraft, armament and electronic equipment under licence from foreign

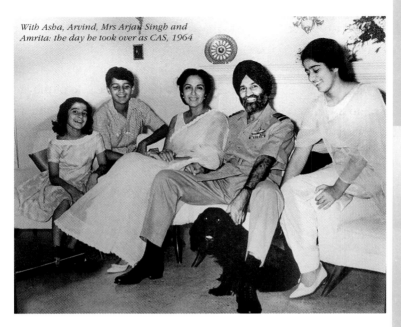

With Asha, Arvind, Mrs Arjan Singh and Amrita: the day he took over as CAS, 1964

companies. "This was to save time as our design capabilities were not up to the mark at that time. Trial and error does take much time and our defence forces should not be allowed to get out of date to enable them to face an enemy equipped with modern weapons. We are now advanced, in producing radar, missiles and helicopters but far behind in producing tanks, aircraft and long-range artillery guns."

Asked to reflect on his tenure as the chief of the IAF, Arjan Singh says he emphasised on training. He is also proud of setting up the Air Force Academy at Hyderabad to train future pilots, and is acutely aware of the problems that have cropped up because of the lack of an advanced trainer aircraft. He also worked at improving the service conditions of the Air Force personnel, especially the flying allowance of the flying personnel. Air Force flying is more strenuous, exacting and risky than civilian flying, yet the Air Force pilots got Rs 400 a month as flying pay, while the civilian pilots were given Rs 400 an hour. Improving the service conditions resulted in the morale of the force shooting up and also helped attract more talented people to join the IAF.

With Air Marshal Asghar Khan CAS, Pakistan in New Delhi, 1964

Working at home — the Air House

Normally, one thinks of the top brass having rather straitjacketed lives, but a cover of *The Illustrated Weekly of India*, December 19, 1965, has a beautiful picture of the Air Chief cycling down a Delhi road with his daughter riding another bicycle. The story behind the picture is quite interesting, as Teji Arjan Singh narrates, "One day our daughter Asha said: 'Oh! Daddy! You don't go cycling with me any longer. You are so busy'."

He said: 'No! Come On! We will go cycling!' He got hold of a servant's bicycle and off they went on the roundabout of Moti Lal Nehru Place. A photographer spotted them, took the photograph and sent it to *The Illustrated Weekly of India*." Overall, Teji certifies that he is a caring husband and father, though his job, especially when he was the CAS, left him with little time for the family.

Cycling with his daughter Asha in 1966

Incidentally, his riding a bicycle was an old story. Even as Air Vice Marshal, Arjan Singh used to often cycle to his office, but he stopped because he felt that cycling was not enough exercise. So he started walking, though that too did not work out since every time he went walking, someone would stop to offer him a lift!

69

CHAPTER FIVE

Diplomatic Sorties

Air Chief Marshal Arjan Singh retired in 1969 at the age of 50. The last aircraft that he flew in the Indian Air Force was a MiG 21. He spent a year or so at 21 Safdarjang Road, Delhi, where he kept busy with family and social engagements.

He was appointed Ambassador to Switzerland in 1971, where he felt at home, having first visited the country in 1938. He loved Switzerland and he used to go skiing there quite often from England. The Indian embassy in Bern had a small staff, less than a dozen

Taking over as Lieut-Governor, Delhi. Present Lieut-Governor, Vijai Kapoor is standing behind

Indian officials, including Chokila Iyer, who was his First Secretary, Political, and later became the Foreign Secretary of India. During his tenure, in Switzerland, the 1971 war with Pakistan, which resulted in the creation of Bangladesh, took place. He explained India's position to the Swiss and also managed to get various kinds of loans and weapons from them. He particularly remembers the Swiss for the fact that they would stick by their word, no matter what.

After presenting his credentials to His Holiness Pope Paul VI, 24 May 1971

Teji Arjan Singh remembers Bern as a quiet place. "In fact, when we were being sent to Switzerland, I thought we would be sent to Geneva. You don't think of Bern as the capital. Switzerland has 26 cantons, or states, and we must have visited at least 20 or 22 of them. In some places we went, they said that the Indian Ambassador has not visited the canton for 20 years! They would ask us with surprise: "Have you been to all the cantons?" To which I would reply, 'Yes,' thinking that the whole country was as big as one Indian state. He used to go to France to play golf by just crossing over the border for that."

He was also concurrently the Ambassador to the court of Pope Paul VI at the Vatican. Pope Paul VI had visited India in 1964 and knew a lot about the country. As Arjan Singh recalls: "We used to have a lot of discussions and he liked me. People often wondered what a military man was doing with a man of peace! He was always very low-key, but was quite interested in India, Pakistan, and East Pakistan (Bangladesh) and the people there. He was concerned about how India would cope with 10 million refugees on its land, and even the kind of problems that would arise

With Lord Mountbatten, in Switzerland, 1972

when so many refugees were be left behind." He had a very bare office, just a simple table, and a few paintings on the wall. When ladies met him, they had to cover their heads.

After a three-year stint in Switzerland, Arjan Singh was appointed High Commissioner to Kenya in 1974. This was a time of flux in Africa since neighbouring Ugandan President Idi Amin had thrown all Asians out of his country, as a result of which the vast Indian diaspora in Africa was feeling rather insecure, with many migrating to the West.

At that time, Kenya was led by Jomo Kenyatta, a distinguished statesman and the first President of independent Kenya. Under

Visiting a multinational company in Switzerland

him, the Kenyans wanted the people of Indian origin to stay, since most were professionals and many of the tea estates were owned by them. In a way, what happened in Uganda created a better environment for Indians in Africa, though many did migrate. Kenyatta was broadminded and even though the freedom movement had started because the best land was with the British and other Europeans, they were not ousted but were asked to stay on. In fact, there were more British living in Kenya 10 years after independence than before it, a tribute to the fair-minded policies of the independent government of a former colonial state.

Ambassador Arjan Singh was quite friendly with President Arap Moi, who succeeded Kenyatta after his death in 1978. "I used to go to his farm in Nakuru, 130 miles from the capital Nairobi. My emphasis was to get to know the local people. Unfortunately, my

Callling on Jomo Kenyatta, the first President of independent Kenya

experience is that various Ambassadors get to know each other better—having parties at each other's places—than the local people. They mostly met among themselves, though they are sent to make contact with the local people and know their issues, problems, etc." While in Kenya, he was also High Commissioner to Seychelles where the Indian community numbered a thousand or so in a population of around 75,000. He partly attributes his success in Kenya to his golf, which he used to play with three or four ministers, as well as several top bankers and industrialists.

At the end of his term as Ambassador to Kenya, the Singhs returned to New Delhi and lived a "retired" life, keeping in touch with their friends and family, and taking care of the children, who had now grown up. They moved to their house in Delhi's diplomatic enclave, Chanakyapuri, and thus began a "holding pattern" when Arjan Singh's day consisted of playing golf and meeting people.

However the kind of experience and ability that he possessed was needed again and again by the government and thus came a stint as a Member of the Minorities Commission (1978-1981). His job was to look after the problems of the minorities in India. As he says of his tenure, "There were not too many problems of the

Teji and Arjan Singh at the Golden Temple, Amritsar, 1966

Sikhs, since by nature they are problem-solvers themselves. However, I must point out that the Muslim community does have many problems of marginalisation." He was also the Chairman of the Indian Institute of Technology (IIT), Delhi, from 1980-1983, where he guided one of the premier technical education institutes of the country.

Asked about his position as a Director of Grindlays Bank for six years, Arjan Singh chuckles and says that it was mainly because he has had an account with the bank since 1935 when he first banked with them in Lahore. Actually, it was more a tribute to his multifarious achievements and the larger-than-life presence that he lent to the boardrooms.

When the anti-Sikh riots took place, he along with other prominent Punjabis like journalist-diplomat Kuldeep Nayar and writer Patwant Singh, formed a joint forum and went to the then President Giani Zail Singh on November 1, 1984, to ask him to call out the Army without delay. "He attempted to contact the Prime Minister and the Home Minister but without success. Unfortunately, the deployment of the Army was delayed till the evening. As a result, many lives were lost. It was a politically inspired situation which went out of control by omission and commission and I do not

At his hobby

blame any particular community for it," he says. Marshal Arjan Singh was actively involved with the relief measures, including disbursement of money to needy persons.

His posting as Delhi's Lieutenant-Governor by the V. P. Singh government near the end of 1989 was the first civil post that Arjan Singh held. He had a competent team and, in fact, the present Lieut-Governor of Delhi, Vijai K. Kapoor, was his Chief Secretary. He is candid enough to admit that he didn't have the depth of knowledge required despite having lived in Delhi for so long. But since he liked to see things for himself, he was able to do much.

At that time there was no elected government and thus the Lieut-Governor had a lot to do. "I was able to help people during my tenure, though I held the post only for a year. It was during this period that the road signs also came up in Punjabi as Punjabis constitute more than 14 per cent of the population of Delhi."

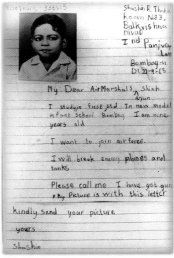

A fan mail during 1965 war

Ever a farmer at heart, he ensured that a fixed minimum rate of compensation be declared for the farmers whose land was bought by colonisers or the Delhi Development Authority. The tenure was a short one since Prime Minister Chandra Shekhar indicated that he wanted his own man as Lieut-Governor and Arjan Singh resigned in December 1990.

CHAPTER SIX

Marshal of the Air Force

When you dismount from your vehicle at a cul-de-sac in Chanakyapuri you can actually hear the birds singing in the heart of Delhi. This is the elite area, bordering a private reserve forest, which time has left untouched. The gate bears a discrete crest of the Indian Air Force on the mailbox. As you look up, right under the skyline there is an exact replica of the Air Force eagle atop the entrance of the house. A lovely vine-covered boundary wall, many well-tended potted plants, a beautifully manicured garden...you

Their present home, 7-A, Kautilya Marg, New Delhi

notice all these as you are escorted in. The trees around the house, and even those on the road in the area, have been planted by Arjan Singh. The imposing doorway is no longer intimidating as you see the welcoming smile of the lady of the house.

You notice a beautiful portrait of Arjan Singh executed in oil in the hall as you enter and on your left is an elegant drawing room where a pristine white dominates the upholstery and even the carpet is white, frightfully difficult to maintain in dusty Delhi. The room is full of bric-a-brac from all over the world—you also see

Marshal of the Indian Air Force Arjan Singh DFC, in his study

the dinning room with a formal setting for 10.

You are ushered into a book-lined study with comfortable leather chairs. The curtains are drawn back and dappled sunlight streams into the room. The scroll of the Padma Vibhushan proudly adorns a wall. The 2.5 kg silver baton of the Marshal of the Indian Air Force is encased in a transparent box and lies on a cabinet. It depicts the Ashoka lionhead with the name and rank inscribed below it, four crests and Ashoka roundals embossed on it.

A water colour painting of the Royal Air Force College, Cranwell, "the oldest Air Force college in the world," hangs near a beautiful teak desk. Marshal of the Indian Air Force Arjan Singh has taken the salute of the passing out parade of the college twice, coincidentally each time six months after the Queen of England had reviewed a similar parade.

You are served tarts and tea. He is at once the host, persuading you to try this and have a bit more of that. Grace matches elegance. Once tea is over, it is back to business again. The mind is sharp, the language precise. He does not need to refer to any notes during the interviews.

You notice the books — a biography of Lord Mountbatten, who had pinned the DFC on the chest of a brave young flyer; bound

Mrs Arjan Singh and Marshal of the Indian Air Force Arjan Singh at their home

works of western classics, a translation of Guru Granth Sahib and, of course, the photo-albums and the flying log book which are under the charge of Teji.

Marshal of the Indian Air Force Arjan Singh has come out with flying colours no matter what life gave him, and most of the time it gave him a good break. He effortlessly transcends stereotypes. This teetotaller gung-ho fighter is not only a committed soldier but also a diplomat. He is wedded to his profession, and also devoted to his family. During his service in the IAF, he has landed on 178

Arvind, Asha, Amrita, Mrs Arjan Singh and Air Chief Marshal Arjan Singh, 28 Sept 1989

airfields and has flown 65 kinds of aircraft and helicopters, the last one being a MiG 21. Even as he has soared in stature and rank, he is famous for keeping his feet on the ground. His competence and leadership have been underscored by his warmth and a genuine interest in his fellow beings. The person behind the persona reinforces the legend. You walk in expecting a larger-than-life person. You walk out after meeting what Y.B. Chavan called a 'jewel'—a legend in his lifetime.

REACTIONS

The announcement that Air Chief Marshal Arjan Singh would be the first person to be given a five-star rank in the Air Force was greeted with a lot of enthusiasm, as can be seen from the following responses:

Defence Minister George Fernandes, in his letter dated January 25, 2002, wrote: "I am glad to inform you that the President has been pleased to appoint you as Marshal of the Indian Air Force with effect from 26 January, 2002. Your outstanding leadership and nurturing groomed the Indian Air Force into one of the best fighting forces in the world. It was in July 1964 that you were appointed as the Chief of Air Staff and you were the first Chief to be promoted to the rank of Air Chief Marshal in December 1965. The significant changes that you brought about in the structuring and functioning of the Air Force took it towards becoming a strong professional force. Successive generations of officers and men in the Indian Air Force have looked up to you as a father figure. Please accept my heartiest congratulations on your appointment which is a token of gratitude of the nation for your exemplary service to it."

Air Chief Marshal Sir Peter Squire, Chief of the Air Staff, Royal Air Force, wrote: "I was delighted to learn of your recent promotion as Marshal of the Indian Air Force. On behalf of all members of the Royal Air Force, please accept my congratulations on this excellent news. You will have many fond memories from your long association with the Royal Air Force and I am sure your many friends in the United Kingdom will be particularly proud of your achievement. This unique honour is testament to your long distinguished career and marks the respect within which you are held."

Sir Richard Evans and Alan R. Keys Chairman and MD respectively of BAE Systems sent a joint statement: "This is the greatest of tributes to you personally, but also for the Indian Air Force which you so ably served and commanded with great distinction in the 1960s. Indeed, your career remains an inspiration to those who have followed you long afterwards at RAF Cranwell. Your command of the famous No. 1 Squadron of the IAF in war is legendary. The Royal Air Force, with which you trained in the late 1930s, is greatly proud of its long association with the Indian Air Force and it is particularly gratifying that the traditions forged during war and peace are zealously maintained by our two Air Forces whose professional capabilities are the envy of the world."

MILESTONES

Born on April 15, 1919 at Lyallpur.

1939 – Commissioned in IAF.

1944 – Awarded Distinguished Flying Cross.

1947 – Air Officer Commanding, Air Force Station, Ambala.

1948 – Director, Training, Air Headquarters.

1950 – Air Commodore, AOC, Operational Command.

1959 – Air Vice Marshal.

1961 – Air Officer in Charge, Administration, Air HQ.

1963 – Deputy Chief of Air Staff and subsequently
Vice Chief of Air Staff.

1964 – Chief of Air Staff.

1965 – Awarded Padma Vibhushan.

1966 – Air Chief Marshal.

1966 – Chairman of the Chief of Staff Committee.

1969 – Retired from IAF.

1971 – Ambassador to Switzerland and the Vatican.

1974 – High Commissioner to Kenya and Seychelles.

1978 – Member of the Minorities Commission.

1980 – Chairman, Indian Institute of Technology, Delhi.

1989 – Lieutenant-Governor, Delhi.

2002 – Marshal of the Indian Air Force.